BULLY*
OLOGY

RYAN JOHNSON

CONTENTS

INTRODUCTION TO BULLY*OLOGY

Dear Friend,

This book represents over 20 years of hard work, teaching, and training in martial arts. I wanted to take a moment to share some thoughts with you in no particular order about what to expect in this book.

If you have a short attention span, learn more interactively or need individual instruction, make sure to head over to www. JohnsonsATA.com. You can see what we do and read what others say about our program.

This book is intended to help parents and kids who are at their wits end. Bullying comes in many forms and levels of intensity. The classic advice of "just ignore it" has a place, but clearly this advice does not work in many situations and may even allow the problem to escalate. As parents, we can get to a point where we just don't know what to tell our kids. No one should have to feel the despair of seeing their child hurting and not be able to help. Sometimes it's the people charged with protecting our kids who are not helping or recognizing the problem. I want to give you a clear path forward to know that there is something else to try. Bullying isn't forever and it's not the end of the world.

I wrote this book, in part, because someone close to me is autistic. Autistic kids and kids with any kind of disability are far more likely to be bullied. I have taught thousands of students and I've heard more stories than I can remember about bullying. Some have been resolved satisfactorily and others left the victim with long lasting emotional scars. Martial arts is meant to empower the weak and embolden the meek. As a martial arts instructor, my responsibility is to help victims of bullying. Like Uncle Ben told Spiderman, "With great power comes great responsibility."

As you read this book, you may notice that I am critical about teachers and administrators who don't take bullying seriously enough. NOTE: I am friends with MANY teachers, preschool through college. I have many students who are teachers and my wife is a former high school math teacher. MOST teachers really care about their kids. They take bullying very seriously and would go to the ends of the earth to protect their students. I love those teachers. But this book isn't about bullying that can be solved easily. My criticisms in this book are directed solely towards the minority of teachers and administrators who don't consider bullying a problem or are not recognizing it when it occurs.

This has been my first attempt at writing, something I thought I would never be able to do, and I would like to thank my mentors at the Parrella Consultant Group for inspiring me and giving me the confidence to think that I could do something that I would have never imagined.

Sincerely,

Ryan Johnson

Ryan Johnson in Sioux City, Iowa, USA

PS—I wrote and edited this book myself. This is my first book and I'm certain there are some spelling, grammatical, and layout errors. If you find any mistakes, please do me a favor and let me know by sending me an email at info@JohnsonsATA.com. Just let me know the page number, sentence, and mistake, and I'll fix it right way. Thank you for your help! As a martial artist, I'm about results. I favor speed and implementation over procrastination. I wanted to get this information into your hands as quickly as I could.

PPS—If you love this, will you please post a review on Amazon? If you DON'T like it, send me an email, tell me why and I'll give you your money back. My direct email is info@JohnsonsATA. com

Please be kind. I have kids. They are very excited about my first book and read what people say about me online, and so do their friends. There is no sense in dragging innocent kids into something unnecessary. Nobody likes a bully and our world has too much hate in it the way it is. Let's be friends. Cool?

MY STORY

The purpose of this book is to help you and your kids define, talk about, and defeat bullying. I believe that no child deserves to be bullied. No child deserves to be teased for reasons beyond their control. It should be okay for kids to be into other activities, and even weird things. I mean heck, I'm sure I do weird things. I know I do weird things too!

But ultimately, our goal in martial arts is to teach children to stand up for themselves, to be strong, to be proud, and to stand in front of a group and show the world what they can do.

When I was about 9 years old, I did chores and saved my allowance for an entire summer to buy the original Nintendo. Since that day, I was hooked. I loved video games, and like many kids today, I would have spent all of my free time playing them. I read fantasy and science fiction books. I was smaller than most of the kids and was fairly short. During my middle school years, I was very self-conscious about my height. For one year I was "the second shortest boy in my grade." I wasn't overly strong or athletic. I had a very active imagination. I was teased off and on for a variety of reasons. I was teased for reading too much. I was called a "teacher's pet" because I didn't get in trouble and got good grades. I had trained in martial arts since I was 8 years old, but the training didn't help me develop any form of confidence in myself. In fact, I was terrified that I might have to use my training someday to defend myself. I knew I would lose. It even made me somewhat of a target for kids who thought it would be funny to pick on the karate kid. One event that still lingers in my mind happened at football practice in 9th grade. I wasn't in any danger of being asked to participate during the varsity practice, so myself and the other 9th graders and JV team members had some bored down time. I'm not sure how it started, but one of the big 10th grade linemen decided it would be fun to pick on me. I don't recall the conversation, but I remember that he could tell I was mad. He challenged me to a fight, which I certainly did not want to do. He even said he'd let me punch him first and held out his chin. I was so impotently angry that I almost took him up on it. But I was certain that he'd move or I'd miss or something and then I'd be in a fight. He continued teasing me, using my martial arts training as another excuse to pick on me. It even got to the point where he said I could hit him with my helmet to start it. I was sorely tempted, but I knew that nothing good would happen. I left that confrontation thoroughly defeated and embarrassed.

I grew up on a farm. Starting when I was in Kindergarten, I had to ride the bus for over 45 minutes to school every day. Luckily, another boy in my grade, Matt, got on the bus about ten minutes after I did. He was also into a lot of the same sports and other things that I was. We were never best friends, but through the years we spent a LOT of time together. When we were old enough to drive we were still friends and rode together to a lot of the same events and parties. Matt was kind of the leader of our group of friends (small town!) and instigated a lot of the craziness and things that we did. He could be kind of a jerk to "the wierdos," but because I was friends with him, I knew that I just needed to keep my head down and we wouldn't have any problems.

In my sophomore year, we were at a mutual friend's house. Someone brought out two sets of boxing gloves and Matt suggested we box each other in front of everyone. Looking back, it's easy for my adult self to see what kind of person he was. He was bigger than me, stronger than me, and he was confident he'd win. Matt was just a tough farm kid with no training of any kind. Maybe he could sense my lack of confidence in my skills, or maybe he really did think all that "karate stuff" was a joke. He was going to beat up the Karate guy, how funny would that be?

Here we were sitting in the basement living room at Josh's house, watching WrestleMania. WrestleMania was pay per view, so I never got to see one as a kid. But we had all pitched in some money and Josh's parents agreed to order it. This was my chance to see if the Undertaker was going to finally be killed (completely)! I was just sitting on the couch in my jeans and tee shirt drinking a coke, when everything changed. I went from feeling comfortable and excited about the event, to fearfully awkward. I felt Matt's attention turn to me, and soon the attention of the whole group was on me. So much for keeping my head down. I didn't know what to do or say to escape the situation. Every option led to embarrassment or worse.

I didn't want to do it. In fact, once I realized what was going on, I was terrified. I said all the right things. "I don't want to", "I don't have anything to prove", "You're right, I'm sure you'll win."

Every objection I had was met with teasing, overcoming my objections, and making me sound like a baby. Most of my "friends" around us were pushing for it to happen, and my one or two real friends were quiet, most likely afraid of drawing attention to themselves or not realizing the seriousness of the situation.

I had been training in martial arts for 8 years. I knew that I should not use martial arts for everyday fighting purposes, but eventually I couldn't stand it! I said, "Okay, let's do it." I tried acting non-nonchalant. I put the gloves on, and when I turned to face Matt he started dancing around, Muhammad Ali style. His palms were facing towards him and his hands were making circles in the air. I could tell immediately that not only was his goal to embarrass me, but also he was going to try to knock me out in front of everyone. And I'm sure this would make a great story for him to boast about. He could forever after tell everyone how he beat up the karate guy. I knew that this was going to be talked about forever and that no one would ever forget how "dumb" all of my years of training had been.

I had zero confidence. At the time, I trained in a style of martial arts that was a lot of fun. I was fairly good at it, but at no time did we learn how to punch to the head or defend a punch to the head; in fact, we didn't even practice keeping our hands up by our faces in a "fighting" situation. But, there were some basic principles that I understood… one of which flashed through my mind. So, I glued my hands to my cheeks, crouched down a little bit, and moved forward. The wannabe Muhammad Ali was dancing around and got a little more serious as I got closer.

And before any other actions, I covered my head an in a fearful state, a sliver of my training kicked in. Even before I was in range for him to punch me, I faked a jab at his head with my left hand. He brought his hands up. With my right hand, I punched him in the stomach. I punched him hard. He slowly walked backwards groaning and sat down on a couch; he removed the gloves without saying a word, set them down on the couch, got up, and walked upstairs. All I recall after that was an amazing feeling of strength, having stood up for myself. The year before I had been humiliated in a similar situation. Now everyone thought I was an amazing super ninja. My friends kept telling me, "Next time there's a fight, I'm bringing you!" That felt amazing! I never wanted to fight again, but for the first time in my life, I felt like I could, if I needed to. After many years, I really could stand up to a bully and make him or her leave me alone. Since then, I've continued training martial arts my entire life; I now own a full-time martial arts academy. Over the last 15 or so years, we've taught thousands of kids, hundreds or thousands of who have been bullied. I've been teaching for nearly 30 years. I've seen and felt the aftermath of what happens when kids are bullied, and I want to prevent it, if possible, without hard punches to the stomach.

I firmly believe that not every child needs to be the basketball or football star. It should be totally okay to be on the chess club, and a kid shouldn't have to worry because he or she enjoys playing chess instead of shooting or passing a ball. It should be okay to get "A's" and enjoy practicing math. It should be okay to be smaller than everybody else, it should be okay to be taller than everybody else, it should be okay to be skinny, and it should be okay to be larger than everybody else. It should be okay to have long or short hair, it should be okay to have the newest name-brand clothes, and it should be okay to have your brother and sister's hand-me-downs.

Kids don't deserve to feel fear of being bullied in school. They deserve to be able to go to school and learn in a safe and friendly atmosphere. Kids deserve to be able to explore any sports and clubs and opportunities and interests that they desire, without fear and without being worried continually about being picked on and being bullied. That's the purpose of the book. I want to give you the tools and lessons that I've learned personally. These are the lessons that we can teach to our kids and to our students to help them overcome bullying and be able to stand up to the world.

DEFINITION OF BULLYING

We all know that bullying is a big problem. Or at least it seems that we should know that bullying is a big problem. However, an interesting thing happened to me when I started teaching a bully proof class at my martial arts academy. This class is specifically designed to teach kids how to deal with bullies in a non-violent way, using martial arts training. Now, the interesting fact is these are all kids who are in a class to teach themselves to be bully proof. You would think they would be very aware of bullies. When I first started teaching this class, I asked them, "Has anybody seen any bully behaviors at school recently?"

Nobody raised their hand. Ten or 15 kids were in this class, and I thought maybe they were just a little bit shy. I said, "Well, who's ever seen bullying at school?" No hands went up. And so I asked, "Who's the kid in your class that maybe is a little different or a little weird that people pick on or call names?" And nobody raised their hand. After talking to them individually during and after class, I realized these kids have been through bully sensitivity training at school, and yet they actually think bullying isn't happening.

Statistically, we know that one in four kids is a victim of bullying in school. How can it be possible that all these kids claim to have never seen it before? The problem lies with an incorrect interpretation or definition of bullying, and my goal is to better define this nebulous term of bullying. I believe that many people think of bullying as being punched or kicked, getting swirlies, or being locked in a locker.

Google defines bullying as "USE: Verb: to use superior strength or influence to intimidate someone typically to force him or her to do what one wants." That sounds like a very forceful and physical form of bullying, and although correct, it's not perfect. I think many forms of bullying are not encompassed by that definition. The following words, I think, paint a better picture: persecute, oppress, tyrannize, browbeat, harass, torment, intimidate, strong arm, and dominate. Those are some examples of words that encapsulate the concept of bullying.

I believe that there should be a broader definition of bullying. Actions like incessant teasing and constant name-calling are also forms of bullying. I don't think bullying has to be trying to make somebody DO something. Going out of your way consistently and regularly to make somebody feel bad or to hurt their feelings is another common form of bullying. That's maybe even more common and I think that's a form of bullying that kids are not recognizing.

One form of bullying that often goes unrecognized is excluding someone from a group. I am reminded of a time that my daughter was hurt in this way. She was in a group of 4 or 5 "good friend." They did lots of things together and spent a lot of time at each other's houses. Then one day, my daughter started crying. When I asked why, she told me that the other girls had planned to go to the mall together, which is very near our house, and hadn't told her. She only found out through "the grapevine." I consoled her and suggested that maybe there was some reason, or maybe they just forgot or something. I suggested that she ask the girl in the group that she was closest with. The next day my daughter was in tears again. She had been told that the reason she wasn't invited was because Emily and Jessica didn't like her anymore. No reason why. They just didn't like her and so she wasn't invited along any more. It broke my heart that kids could be so mean.

I believe that's a form of bullying. I think excluding others just to make them feel bad is absolutely a form of bullying and I think that it can be hurtful, painful, and long lasting like physical bullying. This could be called psychological bullying.

It's important that we can define bullying. On the other hand, I think that some people have too wide of a definition of bullying. When somebody makes you mad, it's not necessarily bullying. When somebody steps on your foot, it's not necessarily bullying. When someone calls you a name, it's not necessarily bullying. Just because somebody doesn't like you or says something about you that you don't like, doesn't mean he or she is a bully. If someone throws something at you or punches you, *even that* doesn't mean that it's bullying. I think those things all can be forms of bullying behaviors, but only when it's done consistently and intentionally to cause you bad feelings. And I think the missing ingredient for those people who cast too wide of a net is that it needs to be something that's happening *consistently* and *regularly*.

In fact, I believe that casting too wide of a net and calling things bullying that really are not that severe harms the case of those kids who actually are being bullied. It's a bit of the boy who cried wolf. I think when you cry bullying for things that are maybe normal everyday kid stuff or things that are a one-time deal, it harms the people around you because it makes people less sensitive to it.

So, what is a proper definition of bullying then? I agree with Google, and it's helpful to list things that could be bullying behaviors. However, I think a better definition of bullying is

Doing physical or verbal acts intentionally and regularly to cause pain or hurt feelings.

The secret is the word *regularly*. There are things that can be bullying behaviors that may or may not be bullying depending on the specific context. So, let's explore that a little bit farther. For instance, if one person or one child punches another, is that bullying? There's many cases where two kids get upset with each other and one of them punches the other. Now, it's never okay and it's never right, but I don't think that I would call that bullying. However, if a child punches another child two or three days in a row after school, that's absolutely bullying. Or if they use it in a way to intimidate and threaten, that's bullying. For instance, a statement such as, "On Friday after school, I'm going to beat you up," is absolutely bullying.

But let's talk about some less extreme examples. What about punching somebody on the arm or (and this happened to me in middle school) flicking someone's nose? Now, I don't like it when people punch my arm and I don't like it when people flick my nose. And, coincidentally, with my 25 years of martial arts training, people don't flick my nose anymore. As you read previously, I was teased, picked on, and bullied as a kid. Now, 20 years later, things have changed. I am now officially a Master of Taekwondo and an advanced practitioner of Brazilian Jiu-Jitsu. I am an avid weight lifter and try to keep myself in peak physical condition. I still read a lot. I still enjoy video games when I have time. I watch all of the super hero movies and do many of the same things I enjoyed when I was younger. The last time I saw one of my bullies was at a wedding of a mutual friend. He didn't recognize me at first and I was hesitant to even let on that I knew him. But eventually he figured out who I was, and we spent a good 2 hours talking. By the end, he apologized for how he had treated me as a kid.

So, if I'm in sixth grade and an eighth grader punches my arm, it's wrong and they should be held accountable for that, but I don't think that necessarily becomes bullying. If they pinch my nose or flick my nose, it's wrong and they should be held accountable, absolutely, but I don't think it's necessarily bullying. When it happens multiple times and it's used to intimidate and harass, then absolutely it's bullying.

What about even lesser examples, less extreme examples. Name calling, when does name calling become bullying? Friends even name call each other, and that's certainly not bullying. Somebody might get mad and call somebody else a name, and that's wrong, but it's probably not bullying. But again, when it happens regularly and consistently to cause hurt feelings, that's when it rises to the level of bullying.

We are going to touch on the issues with zero tolerance at schools in a future chapter. I think that when people become overly sensitive to bullying and call things that are not bullying,

bullying, it desensitizes people. It desensitizes the people around you.

Within schools, bullying is very much a hot button word. It's a buzz word. An incident, disagreement, or altercation at school is handled differently when one of the families brings up the b-word. This difference is in large part due to the fear of lawsuits from families. But, it's important to know that you should understand a proper definition of bullying, which will help you address it more effectively. Actions that may not be bullying aren't acceptable and there should be consequences for them, but we need to use the word 'bullying' when it's due so that we can solve a very, very serious issue for many children.

Equally important to understand is what kind of kids bully others? The answer to this is not as simple as you might think. When I was a kid we were taught that we should feel sorry for the bully (easier said than done!), as they were likely sad on the inside and maybe even bullied at home. While this is undoubtedly true in some cases, it's just one piece of the puzzle. In recent years, we have discovered that many bullies actually have above average self-esteem. They often bully in order to make their circle of friends laugh and to be popular. What they lack is empathy, or an ability to understand the victim's feelings. In some cases, the bully is an otherwise high achieving, happy and popular kid. Sometimes the bully is an otherwise "nice kid" who got swept up or carried away and was not considering the other kid's feelings. And yet other times, the perpetrator really is just a mean little snot.

BEST SELF DEFENSE

In this chapter, I want to give you the secret technique and the ultimate move that will help defeat bullying. This technique is more successful than all other techniques combined. Like we say in our martial arts class it's simple but it's not easy. It's CONFIDENCE. We've talked about who bullies are and what bullying is, but being able to stand up for yourself, with confidence, is your number one form of self-defense.

Let me start with a story. This is a story I heard from my instructor. It's more of a parable, but the truth contained in it is obvious.

Johnny was in 4th grade. He was an average 4th grade boy, getting decent grades and enjoying cartoons and video games. However, he somehow got on the radar of one of the bigger, meaner 5th graders. After school, the 5th grader and his friends would tease and taunt Johnny. After a couple weeks of this, they started following him home, teasing and taunting him the whole way. This was very upsetting to Johnny, but he didn't know what to do about it. Eventually it became physical, with pushing, knocking books out of his hands, and trying to trip him. One day, when things got bad enough, Johnny tried to take another way home. Instead of following the road, he ran through some neighbors' back yards. The bullies followed and, before he could get away, knocked him down. The big bad bully jumped on top of him and sat on him, preparing to torment him further. What neither of them knew was that under his back was a bee. Fearing for it's life, the bee stung Johnny in the back. In a spasm of pain and surprise, Johnny bucked the bully off, jumped to his feet, and ran home. The next day, when Johnny left school, he looked around. The bullies weren't there to follow him. He was able to walk home in peace that day and every day after.

The morale of the story is that it was only when Johnny proved (even unintentionally) that he was able to stand up to the bullies, did they leave him alone. Confidence gives kids that same ability to stand up for themselves and help to stop bullying.

Martial arts teaches the weakest and the meekest among us to have confidence and that's not by accident. Gaining confidence in martial arts is not accidental like it might be with many other activities. It's very intentional. Martial arts is designed to take a student who's lacking confidence and who is physically weak, and develop them into somebody who can stand up for themselves. I'm sure you can think of a time when you've had to stand up for yourself and you were maybe terrified, shaking in your boots and sweating bullets. But when you did it, it worked better then you could have imagined. We all remember Daniel-son from *The Karate Kid* in the All City Tournament. Bullied, picked on, and beaten up throughout the movie, he was terrified and shaking while confronting his nemesis. Yet he was able to find the strength in himself (with Mr. Miyagi's help) to stand up for himself. In the end, he won the day, defeated his nemesis, and the trophy was his.

That's confidence. One way that you can think about the benefit of confidence is to think about predators and prey. Lions, for example, might circle around and around a pack of wildebeests as they stalk them. The problem is the wildebeests are big and strong. The lions have claws and teeth and they're strong too, but they don't just go rushing straight in. They stalk around the edges. The way they decide who to take down is they look for the weakest member of the herd. Why the weakest? Because it's the easiest and bullies are no different. They like to pick on generally the weakest and the meekest, i.e. the people who are not going to fight back.

I've trained at martial arts for most of my life. I train daily in Taekwondo, Jiu-Jitsu, and weapons training. I lift weights in my basement gym three or four days a week, and I'm in the best physical shape of my life. I can tell you that even though I was in martial arts for a long time, I still got bullied in school. Nobody bullies me today. I have tremendous confidence in myself. Confidence is something that people can sense. They can see it in you. The bullies want the weakest member of the herd. The lions will circle around until they find a baby calf or a sick wildebeest, and they'll work hard to get them isolated. I mean, does that sound like real world high school or what? They work to get them isolated so that they can take them down without fear of injury or reprisal. Once they've identified the weakest and isolated them from the herd, they attack.

The best self-confidence is the ability to stand up for yourself, to stand tall, to look the bullies in the eye, to put your finger out, and to say, "You need to leave me alone." We are not wildebeest. Even the weakest among us has the ability to develop this kind of confidence. It is not a forgone conclusion that you will be picked off by the lions of society. It seems amazing. Most bullies are bigger and stronger than you. Like we say in our bully proof class, "They're bigger, stronger, more athletic, faster, and smellier. They have all the advantages." Yet when you stand up for yourself you don't need to necessarily be stronger than the bully, you just need to be stronger than the options that the bully has to pick on you. That's why confidence is so effective. Perhaps you can remember a time when you used confidence to stand up for yourself and if we could give that gift of confidence to kids, well, it could be life changing.

As I mentioned before I grew up on a farm. We always had big farm dogs and I remember a time when one of my dad's friends pulled into the yard. My dog ran up to his truck, but when he opened the door his little lap dog leapt out. It started barking and chasing my big old farm dog! It chased my dog all the way into the garage and then left him there. The little guy went back and jumped in the truck, seemingly completely content in his dominance of the situation. Your kid can be that small dog. Size doesn't matter. It's confidence. In the following chapters we're going to talk about how martial arts specifically teaches confidence and teaches it to the people who need it the most.

BUILD CONFIDENCE LIKE
A VIDEO GAME

One of the best ways that martial arts teaches confidence is through its stepping stone method of making kids better at something. Taking them from zero to greatness. It's a fact that when a child gets really good at anything, it will help build his or her confidence and self-esteem. When a child gets very good at playing the drums or the piano, writing, mathematics, skiing, or horseback riding, his or she develops a greater sense of confidence and self-esteem. I think that martial arts has an edge in this area, and I'm going to tell you exactly why.

Martial arts has a stepping stone method very similar to video games, and as we know, video games are highly addicting to kids. Martial arts is able to capture their attention and build them up from zero to confident in the same way that a video game goes from level zero to level 10. What do I mean by that? When you start a video game, if you got dropped into level 10 right away, in the beginning, it would be too hard. Your skills would not be good enough and you would not enjoy it. If the video game started at level zero, you might enjoy it at first, but if it didn't get any harder, if it didn't become more challenging, you would not continue playing, and you would quickly become bored. A good martial arts academy is the same way.

When your child goes to their first martial arts class, it might be a challenge, but they should leave with their head held high, thinking, "You know what? I think I can do this." Then each day that they go they should be able to see progress, particularly in the beginning when progress is the fastest. Every single time they go to class, they'll see the progress getting better and better and better, and then as they improve, the requirements get harder and more challenging.

Maybe at first, you start off breaking the simplest boards. Then as you become a little stronger from the push-ups and your techniques become better, you start breaking a little bit harder board. Over time you move up to another class and you break even harder boards. As you get older and stronger and more confident, eventually you're breaking the hardest boards. That's the same way that a video game captures a student's imagination at level zero and hooks them all the way up to level 10. Every aspect of martial arts should have this ladder or this stair-step system.

At our academy the techniques that you learn often times go from very basic and simple to learn, i.e. techniques you can learn in only one class, to techniques it would take years to master. Progress moves from simpler things that you can be successful with the first day to things that are extremely challenging and awe-inspiring to people who don't train martial arts.

Even weapons training is the same way. Every kid wants to pick up a pair of nunchucks, and he or she should be able to very early in their career. They want to do things with them that seem really cool and capture imagination. Martial arts captures the imagination of students in a way that other sports just can't do. For us, that's the concept of being a Black Belt. Just like every kid would love to become a ninja, from day one, we plant the idea of what a Black Belt is in our students' minds, and we reinforce that very strongly on a regular basis.

At our academy, we say Black Belts are the BEST and we mean it. The ideal Black Belt is strong and powerful, with his or her head held high, making eye contact with their foes. Their techniques are flawless, their kicks are devastating, and their punches are lightning fast. But not only are Black Belts physically the best, but also, they are the most confident and the most disciplined. They have the highest levels of integrity, focus, and self-control. In essence, a Black Belt is the best of every attribute that we train in our martial arts classes, and then we show the kids the step-by-step method that we're going to use to make them into a Black Belt and into the ultimate warrior.

They can see the progression from day one, and we make it very easy to start. Your first martial arts class should be filled with things that you can accomplish successfully the very first day, and you should leave your martial arts class thinking, yeah, I can do this, this is MY THING. This step-up concept is unique to martial arts. For example, very often parents sign up their kids for one activity after the other. More and more, some kids are in three, four, five activities at a time, and I get it. In today's world, we see people like Venus Williams and Lebron James prodigies from when they were kids, trained from when they were little to become the ultimate at their sport. Every parent dreams of their kids being that successful; in fact, I don't know about you, but I know my kids are going to be that successful if I can just find the activity that they're natural at, and that's what parents our looking for.

In reality, most people never find that one activity they are naturally better at than the rest of the world. In fact, people who are that good very often don't last. Many times, students who are able to accomplish goal after goal without difficulty don't find the reward from those goals to be strong enough. However, martial arts can inspire a student who has tried four, five, ten other activities and quit because they didn't feel like they could be good at them.

When a student joins martial arts, they train from the start. They learn a skill and build confidence from the start. Then the next day, we add a little more and a little more and they move up, join a new class, join a new team, move into the intermediate or advanced class, and join a competition team or an instructor team. Then someday, they look back and they realize how far they've come, and the idea of Black Belt is not that far away.

What actually happens when students get into our Black Belt class is they stop saying every day Black Belts are the best. They start saying Black Belts TRAIN THE BEST because they know that all the lower belts are working hard every day. They know that they've been put on a pedestal. They know that they need to strive to live up to those ideals. They try to meet and exceed this idea of Black Belt, and they know they should keep working hard to stay ahead.

It's this powerful concept that gets in their mind that really inspires kids to excellence. and to want to work hard; it captures their imagination. Ultimately, when we can capture their imagination, then we are able to make them good, and that will build their confidence.

Other sports don't really have the same ability to inspire this image in their mind of excellence. For instance, when you play soccer, do you want to be like Pele? Maybe, but I don't think that has the same idea, the amazingness, the same sense of awe and inspiration as wanting to be a Black Belt.

When you play basketball, do you want to be like Lebron or Michael Jordan? Yeah, they were great, but maybe they're too concrete and it's easy to see that you will never been that good because nobody else ever has been.

Don't get me wrong, Black Belts are better, they're the best, but it's a concept that feels achievable and captures their imagination in way that takes them on this amazing journey that ultimately ends with the development of unshakable, rock solid confidence. That's the first, most important step to self-defense.

This is in contrast to most other kid sports/activities. All kid sports claim to teach "sportsmanship" and other important life skills. However, the meaning of sportsmanship on many teams is simply "don't cry or get mad" and "you MUST go through the high five line at the end and mumble good game to each player." They don't actually teach or talk about sportsmanship or any other life skills that are not directly related to winning. And let's face it, in most sports winning is THE most important thing. Meaning over time, everyone who's not at high skill levels gets left out until they quit. In my martial arts academy, we actively teach those life skills. We teach and practice Discipline, Respect, and Confidence. We practice being mentally tough and resilient. You can learn good things from other sports, but a good martial arts academy is the only place that will actively teach those skills.

STONE WALL

"Sticks and stone can break my bones, but words can never hurt me!"—common

We established previously that confidence is the best form of self-defense. But why is that? I think that very often bullying can fly under the radar and not get taken as seriously as it should be. However, I also think on the other end of the spectrum there's times when people jump the gun and become overly sensitive or overly offended and call bullying when maybe it's not. This is another great opportunity to talk about why that confidence is such a great form of self-defense.

You can imagine a student who is very shy and introverted with low self-esteem. Maybe this is you or your child, and when somebody calls him or her a name, it hurts his or her feelings. We've all been called things before that hurt our feelings. Maybe this student gets called a name or maybe he or she gets a disliked nickname. I can understand how aggravating that would be to be called something that you don't like. Now is that bullying? Yeah I think it very much could be. But I can also imagine a student on the other end of the spectrum, maybe one of the big confident football players. If I had tried to call him a name, he would have just thought I was dumb or laughed in my face because it didn't hurt his feelings. He is so confident that no amount of name-calling could shake his self-esteem: that's the Stone Wall.

So you can imagine children who are called names or picked on in a sort of under the radar fashion. If we could develop their confidence to that high level maybe they too can say, "You know what, that doesn't even bother me. That's a dumb name. You're dumb that you think that, and it doesn't hurt my feelings at all." I guess as an adult we would say, "To have thick skin." As an adult that's an important part of being a grown up, having thick enough skin to take an insult or to take a criticism and to not get upset. If we can give that gift, that thickness of skin, that mental fortitude to a child, it's an amazing gift.

Consider a medieval castle. The walls are made of wooden poles stacked around your city. When the bullies show up with their catapults launching rocks at your walls, they'll easily bust holes through the wood. But if you could take those walls and built them up with stone to make them taller and thicker, when the bullies show up and start slinging the same stones you barely even notice and don't need to do anything to react. That is the reason that we teach confidence to kids. Confidence should be a Stone Wall defense.

GIFT OF LOSING

There's another important way that martial arts teaches confidence to kids, and that's with the gift of losing. That seems ridiculous. Why would I call losing a gift? Well, losing in the right circumstances can be a tremendous confidence builder in the long run.

In our Academy, we have a student who is a legend. This guy was amazing. At 16 years old, he was like Midas; everything that he touched simply turned to gold. I could show him a technique that took me two years of training to get good at, and he would do it the same day. When we're talking about martial arts tricks, there is high-level skills like 540s, 720s, and Butterfly Twists (really impressive martial arts tricks!). This guy could do it all. In fact, it was really too easy for him.

He was so good at it, that after a while he stopped attending classes regularly. When he was older, junior/senior level in high school, he got a girlfriend and we didn't see him very often. That's not unusual at that age. But then, about once a year he would come back and train more consistently just in time for the Regional Tournament, where we bring in competitors from five or six states. It's a pretty big deal.

This guy, I'll call him Steve, was physically amazing, and when he would hear that the tournament was coming around, he would get re-motivated and would come back to class for a few weeks. And then he would compete, and inevitably, he would get first place. In fact, Steve was so good that he would often win his matches 5-0 or 5-1 while doing some crazy kicks that most people would never attempt in competition. This went on for a couple of years, and every tournament season I kept hoping that he would lose, not because I want my students to lose and I want somebody to be emotionally hurt, but because I wanted him to see that it can't be that easy. And yet for him, it was. This regional competition wasn't hard enough for him. The next step up in competition is District Championships. In our organization, you earn points by placing at regional competitions. At the end of the tournament season, if you are in the top ten in your division, you earn an invitation to District Championships. And if you win at Districts, you automatically qualify to compete to be World Champion!

Because winning was too easy for him, Steve was never motivated to put in the effort to go to enough tournaments to get the points necessary to get the invitation to Districts. And it would have been easy for him. It just wasn't a big enough challenge to inspire or motivate him. Finally, one tournament season, by a bit of luck, he went to one extra tournament. At his two tournaments that season, he happened to meet up with three other district top ten competitors, and he won. This meant that he prevented them from earning the points from that event and without really trying he made it onto the bottom of the Top Ten list, earning an invitation to Districts.

We didn't see him regularly again for a while, but as Districts got closer Steve started coming to more classes again. He was getting excited for his shot at becoming District Champion and competing at World Championships. He was finally feeling that motivation. People had been telling him since he started that he could be World Champion if he wanted, and now he wanted to.

Steve trained really hard the two or three weeks before Districts. In his first match, he fought like normal, doing unpredictable, crazy things and won fairly easily. But the second round was different. His competitor was just as fast as him, just as flexible, and very strategic. Steve got caught while doing some out-of-the-ordinary kicks and was quickly down 3-1. Time to get serious. Steve did come back and tie it up at 4-4, but as the clock was winding down his opponent scored on him with a simple punch. He showed great sportsmanship afterwards. Steve shook his opponents hand, told him he did a great job, and clapped for all of the competitors to come after him. He stayed and cheered on his teammates for the remainder of the tournament and seemed in good spirits when he left.

However, after he lost, we didn't see Steve again. He was so demoralized he didn't have the fire anymore to train. He was so demoralized by his loss that it just wasn't worth it anymore. This guy could have been the best of the best. He could've been a World Champion, he could've owned martial arts academies, and he could've gone on to play sports in college; he was actively recruited to play soccer and golf in college on scholarship. He had seemed like King Midas, where everything he touched or tried to do turned to gold. But reality is harsh. If he had lost earlier in his career, if he had learned that failure is part of the process of winning, maybe things might have turned out differently. In the end, he chose not to accept any scholarships or play any further sports. He now bounces around in some various construction jobs and I'm sure he's great at that too. He stops by the academy a couple of times a year and does a class or two, but has not had the fire since then. I don't think that one tournament led to a life of wasted potential. However, it illustrates my point that losing, learning to lose and overcome obstacles is good for kids and should not be put off until they are an adult.

This guy was amazing, and yet he's far, far from the most accomplished student that we have. I want to contrast him with another student from our jujitsu class. Jujitsu is more of a wrestling-based style, i.e. grappling. The beauty of jujitsu is that we can verify and test the techniques. For example, we can train much closer to real life intensity than we can in taekwondo class. In training, people can't punch and kick each other full bore all the time. People will get hurt. There's no way to train that way. In jujitsu, however, as long as both parties are being safe, they can perform the techniques at full power in a real attempt to put their competitor/partner in a position where they have to submit or give up.

One of my close friends and best jujitsu students was a white belt for about a year, which is pretty standard. For this story I'll call him Mark. He tested for his next belt, the blue belt, and joined the big dog class: the advanced class, the master cycle class. For every student, this is a very exciting time when get to learn the advanced high-level techniques.

They begin sparring on a much more regular basis with people who are really, really good. When you lose in jujitsu and you submit, it's called getting tapped out, and this guy got tapped out. A lot. In fact, he was unable, for the longest time, to submit any of his partners in class. Mark was smaller than many of the rest of the people, so most of his training partners were bigger and heavier and had the strength and weight advantage.

Because he was the newest student in that class, all the students at that time in that class knew more techniques than him and had been training and sparring longer, and he was submitted over and over and over, for months. Gradually he started holding his own a little more, and even catching submissions now and then, but over this time he became somewhat frustrated.

We would have conversations after class about how he didn't feel like he was progressing, and he didn't feel like he was getting any better, and he didn't think he could remember anything. In jujitsu, it takes a long time to become a blue belt, so there was a stretch of time where we didn't have any new, advanced students joining that class.

And sometimes they would join, sometimes they would come, and then they would fade out after a while, probably due to the same thing that happened with the Steve. Once they realized that it was difficult, it wasn't worth the effort any more. About a year later we had a handful of 3, 4, 5, 6 new blue belts who were a lower rank than Mark, and he started really catching people and submitting them.

Mark said to me, "Yeah, Mr. Johnson, but I'm only submitting the people who are brand-new." And I would say, "Yes, my friend. That's because that's exactly what happened to you. They all submitted you because you were newer, and now you're doing it to them. Doesn't that tell you that you're progressing?"

And when we would talk about it, Mark could agree

somewhat that he was progressing, but he still had a low opinion of his own skills. It wasn't until probably his second year in the jujitsu class, when we had 10 or 20 people below him and only a handful people who were significantly more knowledgeable, when he started to realize, "I'm pretty good."

People started saying things like, "Man, I never catch that guy." Or, "That guy's so technical I'm lucky if I survive and don't get submitted." Or, "Man, I get caught by that guy five times every match." After a while, Mark started to realize that all his hard work had paid off, and he never became conceited or arrogant, but he stopped denigrating his own skills and started feeling the confidence that he deserved from his hard work.

Now I really believe that all of that losing was good for my friend, and I think it primed him to be able to appreciate and to have the well-deserved confidence when he started getting better, improving, and finally winning. When students compete, whether it's in class or in a tournament competition, martial arts gives them an opportunity to lose in a way that can lead to greater confidence.

It lets them lose in a way that's not, hopefully, earth-shattering and demoralizing, but in a way that can inspire them to work harder, to train harder, and to try to be better. And then, once they are better and they overcome those obstacles, they can feel that well-deserved confidence like my friend.

And that confidence, again, is the best and most effective self-defense. I think that my friend would tell you that the confidence that he's developed through his martial arts training will be more effective than all the techniques put together.

EVOLUTION

L et's talk about evolution. You know the kind of evolution where fish turn into monkeys and monkeys turn into people. And, it's not quite that simple but you get the idea. The concept behind evolution is survival of the fittest. For example, pretend there are two creatures or maybe a whole population of animals. Some of them have a gene that causes their coloring to be a little more camouflage and others have a coloring that causes them to be a little less camouflage. Over time, the ones that are a little less camouflaged are more often eaten by predators, and the ones that are a little more camouflaged are less often eaten by predators. The more camouflaged creatures will survive longer and have more offspring. And of course, over time that will lead to the more camouflaged animals becoming the more common, if not the only, form of that species.

That's a simplified version of evolution, but it can help understand bullying. I think that part of the reason that bullying often gets worse is because of a kind of social evolution. We talk in our classes about how bullies are very smart. They fly under the radar. They often do enough to cause harm to the victim but not enough to get caught. They're very aware of what those levels are.

For instance, the kind of bullying you might experience in the classroom is a person tapping his or her pencil in a certain way that's irritating to you. Or a person saying certain phrases he or she knows you don't like or calling you a name you hate. That might fly under the teacher's radar as everyday kid behaviors. And the kind of bullying that you might have after school might be different because it's not supervised. It might be more physical.

I believe that bullies learn this over time through a type of evolution. For instance, when a kindergartener doesn't like another kid, they might hit him or her. And of course, when that happens then the child doing the hitting gets in trouble. Next time, they might decide that hitting is not a good idea. He or she will express anger emotionally or verbally, not physically, to avoid getting in trouble while continuing to hurt the victim.

Bullies learn to get away with a lot of stuff by figuring out where the limits are and flying under the radar. Over time they hone their skills and become more sophisticated. It's not a conscious decision. They subconsciously learn exactly where the limits are based on their surroundings and their victims, and they know where the supervision is that could get them caught. Bullies know how far they can push things without getting in trouble.

They are also very good at doing it out of sight of teachers. Kids who are not bullies are not always aware of the teacher's focus and attention, but bullies who are focused on picking on someone are well aware of where the teacher's attention is, and they know when they can get a chance to get away with whatever they're planning. Just think back to the old days of spitballs in class.

Not only are they aware of the teacher's attention, and use their every opportunity to bully, they're also aggravatingly good liars. This has probably been honed over years and years of bullying to find the excuses that work the best to get out of trouble. Through simple evolution of their language, they get better and better at getting out of trouble. One of the things that I hear the most from my students is that when they get picked on, as soon as they tell the teacher, the other person says, "Yeah, but they were doing the same thing back to me."

Or maybe the bully might say, "Yeah, but they did this first," even if that's not true. In some cases, the bullies will even pick up on the fact that the victim is fed up with their bullying and is about to tell the teacher, and they'll go tell the teacher first. They'll tell the teacher that the victim was actually the one who was name calling, fighting, or whatever it is. They've learned, I believe, through evolution of their language to find the excuses that keep them out of trouble the best. So, I think that bullies over time become better and better at using zero tolerance in their favor. It's understandable why a teacher may not recognize the continuing nature of the bullying. It's also understandable why a teacher may not want to call it bullying. Maybe you were picked on when you were a kid and you turned out okay. That's great. That doesn't mean that this kid deserves to be picked on like you were.

The bully's evolution even extends to how they choose their victims. A few times in his or her life, a bully may inadvertently choose a victim that will eventually stand up for him or herself. But after several years of practice, they get very good at choosing victims that will give them the response they are looking for and not fight back. As bullies gain more experience, they seem to be able to find the person most susceptible to their attacks very quickly. Our goal with building confidence is for our child to no longer reside in that "potential victim" zone.

Kids with the bully gene or the bully personality don't intentionally try to figure out how to be the most effective bully. I think that over time that is essentially what happens. They hone their skills. They get better and better. They have this bullying personality and over time, they're able to bully much, much more effectively and get into less trouble because they have the two competing goals: 1) cause as much harm to the victim as I can, but 2) don't get into trouble myself.

This is part of why it is very difficult for some teachers to recognize or to catch bullies in the act. It can be hard for the victims to be able to prove their case. Often with these kinds of bullies it comes down to "he said-she said." If the bully is good at his or her job, so to speak, they always have plausible deniability. Like *Mission Impossible* they always have an alternate explanation for what happened. The victim says, "Hey teacher, Johnny bumped into me again," and then of course the answer is, "Well it was just an accident. I didn't mean to." Or, "Johnny knocked the books out of my hands," or, "No, somebody else pushed me and so I bumped into him. It wasn't my fault." Or, "Johnny called me a name first." Or, "We were just fooling around and I didn't say anything mean." The excuses can go on and on. It makes it difficult for the victim to get the help that they need as the bullies get better and better.

Over time, some bullies get good at deniability and can effectively fly under the radar. They choose their victims successfully and torment them for long periods while staying under the radar and not getting in much trouble. The teachers may even know that they're bullies and that they're mean and that they're picking on the other kid but for the sake of not being confrontational, if they have a good excuse, then it's hard to really crack down on them.

We talked in a different chapter about teachers. For some teachers it's hard to have that confrontation with parents that stick up for their bullying kid no matter what. And when the kid has plausible deniability, they know that mom and dad will back them up and that teachers are not going to be confrontational. The evolution of bullying, therefore, encompasses not only the bully, but also the surrounding community.

REAL SELF DEFENSE

We talked in a previous chapter about how getting good at any skill can build confidence and self-esteem in a child, giving them a better chance to stand up for themselves. But, why is martial arts better than getting really great at soccer or baseball? I mean, I guess you could defend yourself with a baseball bat, but no of course that's not it. It's because martial arts are designed for self-defense and when you're training to be good at self-defense that will give you the confidence to stand up for yourself.

Now let's just talk about the training itself. A good martial arts academy is going to train in a very fun and exciting way. It should be like a game. It should be as fun as going to soccer practice. It should be as fun as going to a baseball game or playing football. In fact, for a lot of kids we can deeply capture their imagination. It's better than those activities because they buy into its real-world usefulness. It's an outlet that allows them to be physical, to express themselves, and to have a great time doing something that's exciting and interesting. At the same time, a good martial arts academy is going to teach these things in a way that's realistic.

When I was a kid, we were taught a lot of things that were not realistic. I told this story earlier about my friend finding the boxing gloves and challenging me to a fight. The problem that I had is at the time I had been training in martial arts for probably eight years. That's a long time and in today's world, somebody who trains in martial arts for eight years should be extremely effective and deadly. But at the time, I was not. Not only did I lack confidence in my physical skills, but also I knew that a lot of the things I had been taught were not real. Even though I was very good at a physical activity, I knew that I didn't know how to fight and I wouldn't be able to defend myself. In fact, we were taught a lot of things back then like using our feet, crescent kicks for instance, to knock guns out of people's hands. We learned jumping kicks that look great in demonstrations but have no place in real self-defense.

Now all that stuff is fun. We teach jump kicks too, and we teach craziness, but it's important that a martial arts academy teaches realistic self-defense techniques. It's important to separate those fun-tournament-crazy-artistic moves from the realistic self-defense. In today's world, we have such a tremendous benefit from the UFC. Whether you like the UFC or not, the value is it's a real proving ground of what kinds of things work and what really can happen when two people are fighting each other. This has allowed us over the years to distill down and to find out the things that people really need to know to defend themselves. In our kids' classes, we teach realistic self-defense, whether that's Taekwondo with punching, kicking, and developing confidence, or whether that's jujitsu class with our grappling techniques. We're teaching the same things that we see are effective in the ring and out in the street.

I honestly believe that kids can sense when things are getting too crazy and not realistic. Kids can sense when they learn something in class that won't remotely work when they show their friends; they can tell up to a point what's real and what's not. Now some people fall for charlatans and some people believe in crazy things (like fake moon landings), but I think that most people are effective at sensing what's real and what's not. For kids, it's important to know the difference between what looks cool and what can be useful for self-defense.

In the next chapter, we'll talk about what happens when it does come time to throw down, take the gloves off, and physically stand up for yourself.

FIGHTING

O
kay, now it's time finally to talk about fighting, and I mean actual fighting. First, I want to tell you what we teach our students, and I want to give you some actual outcomes that we've had of students in the past who have physically defended themselves. The first thing I want you to know about our approach to fighting is that fighting is always, always the last resort.

I want to give credit to my mentor and the leader of the ju-jitsu martial art that we follow: Rener Gracie. This information comes direct from our Gracie Bully Proof class, which has five rules of engagement.

Rule number one: Avoid the fight at all costs.

Rule number two: If physically attacked, defend yourself.

Rule number three: If verbally attacked, follow the three T steps (I'll describe the three T steps in a moment).

Rule number four: Never punch or kick the bully. Establish control and negotiate.

Rule number five: When applying submissions, use minimal force and negotiate.

We say these rules out loud in every single Bully Proof class, and our students are required to recite them in order to test for a new belt. They become so ingrained, that all of our students can say them at any time. The first point of these five rules of engagement is to give kids an understanding and a confidence of when they should not use physical self-defense to defend themselves. But the rules also establish the confidence to know when the time is right and necessary to defend oneself. These students know when they are in the right, they know their parents will stand up for them, and they know their martial arts academy and instructors will support them 100%.

An understanding of these steps is critical in today's age of zero-tolerance because children may be well aware that they're going to get in trouble. And yet, these five rules of engagement will help keep them out of trouble and give them the knowledge that even if they do get in trouble, what they did was right. These five rules are designed, as I said, to help keep kids out of trouble.

After we recite these rules, we ask their parents to talk with them on the way home and explicitly tell the child that if it becomes necessary they are authorized to physically defend themselves with jujitsu. Now, keep in mind that the jujitsu that we teach is completely nonviolent. You saw one of the rules is never punch or kick the bully; there is no striking involved. But it's important for kids to have that authorization, and know that if it's necessary they should defend themselves.

Imagine the worst-case scenario. If your child gets punched in the face, is he or she required to take another hit or are they authorized to defend themselves? Now as parents, we can understand why the schools teach that kids should tell the teacher, tell mom and dad, and try to make friends with the bully. We agree with all those things and we've talked about them in other chapters.

But as adults, we understand that things do sometimes rise to a level where you must stand up for yourself. When our kids get to that level, we want them to have the confidence to stand up tall and to be able to defend themselves without hurting themselves or the other person. As a parent, we understand why the schools can't teach kids to physically stand up for themselves.

But the reality is sometimes physical defense is necessary. And if you're not willing to stand up for yourself when necessary, the bullies will realize that and capitalize. You'll be the weakest wildebeest in the herd.

So now I want to break down the five rules of engagement. I'd like to explain what they are, how we teach them, and give you some ideas of how we use this to keep kids out of trouble.

Rule number one:

Avoid the fight at all costs, and we really do mean at all costs. If the bad guy wants to fight you and they call you a chicken, or if they're calling you names and they're making you angry and mad, you need to avoid the fight at all costs.

You need to tell your teacher or you need to tell your mom and dad. In fact, in the beginning of our Bully Proof class, we tell kids that they need to tell their parents every time they get bullied because their parents will be the ones to help them determine when it's time to stand up for themselves. And your parents will never give you the authorization unless they know that you're being bullied.

It's important for kids to tell their parents, and for parents to be receptive to listening. We do really want them to avoid the fight at all costs. We want them to exhaust every avenue of help that's possible. However, parents and kids need to remember Rule number two.

Rule number two:

If physically attacked, defend yourself. This is one that we ask parents on a regular basis to tell their kids that, "Yes, this is true." If you're physically attacked, defend yourself.

If somebody punches you or kicks you, it should be obvious, but to kids it's not. If somebody punches you or kicks you, use jujitsu to defend yourself. Typically in our jujitsu class, this would mean a basic takedown technique controlling them on the ground until they either give up or become exhausted. Then only if necessary, applying a submission technique to force them to give up and capitulate, but this also goes a little bit farther. Kids ALWAYS have the right to protect themselves.

There are many actions and behaviors that we call "kids being kids," but we shouldn't accept behaviors from kids that we as adults would never accept. As an adult man, I would never allow somebody to punch my arm more than once. I would never allow somebody to twist my nose, pinch my arm, flick my ear, poke me in the chest, kick my shins, or knock my books out of my hands on a regular basis. If you're physically attacked, you are authorized to defend yourself.

Rule number three:

If verbally attacked, follow the three T steps: talk, tell, and tackle. Now, who do we talk to? First, talk to the bully. This is usually overlooked by most kids, and for most kids it would be easier if we didn't tell them to do this. Most kids would prefer to duck their head and tell mom and dad or the teacher. They would often prefer to move on to part two of this rule, which I'll explain next. It is very difficult, maybe almost impossible, for many kids to stand up tall, to look the bully in the eye, and to tell them to stop. However, we teach that until you've done that, you are not authorized to initiate any physical techniques such as taking them down and making them stop. Kids ALWAYS have the right to defend themselves against physical attacks, but against verbal attacks, they MUST tell them unequivocally to STOP.

So talk, tell, and tackle. Talk to the bully. Stand up tall, look him in the eyes, and tell him, "You better leave me alone," or "You need to leave me alone." Tell your parents and tell the teachers. Unless it's a physical attack that needs to be dealt with right now, you must tell the parents and tell the teacher before going any further and attempting any other physical defenses on your own.

Your parents and your teachers are the adults in your life—if this is happening at school—who are most capable of helping you and stopping the bully, and most teachers take that job very seriously. Your parents are the people who love you the most of everyone in this entire world, and they're the ones that will go to bat for you.

Not every kid is always completely convinced that their parents can or will help them, and we try to drive home the point of just how seriously your parents want to help you. In fact, the kids who are in our Bully Proof class are there because their parents want to help. Sometimes we'll say, "If you were in the backyard and got attacked by a saber-toothed tiger, your best friend will probably run away, and actually that's the wise choice." But your parents are the people in this world who would run out of the house and leap on the saber-toothed tiger's back and attack them with their bare hands in order to help you. That's how much they love you, that's how much they care about you, and that's how far they would go to help you if you're being bullied. So talk, tell, and tackle. Tell your parents and tell the teachers. Then tackle.

First, we're going to tackle them verbally, and this is something that only typically comes after receiving your parents' permission. Like my friend in law enforcement said, "You know what? Today's the day. We've had enough, we've tried everything, it's time for you to stand up for yourself." We're going to tackle them verbally first, and here's precisely how we do it.

This is a little bit of amazing psychological warfare, and it's important to understand that many times bullies are bullying either because they think it's funny, or very commonly, to make their friends and the people around them laugh and be funny. So when a student stands up for himself, he's going to say, "Look, bully. You pick on me every day. You call me names, you hit me, you kick me, you knock the books out of my hand, and this has been going on all year. Are you challenging me to a fight?"

This is much deeper than it sounds like because this puts the ball in the bully's court and forces them to do one of two things. It forces them most likely to say "no," and bullies are smart, they'll do it in a way to save face. They'll say, "No, you're not worth my time," or, "It's not worth it." But when the victim has stood up for him or herself and looked the bully in the eye and asked if he or she is challenging him or her to a fight, and the bully backs down, the victim is authorized to say, "If you're afraid to fight me, then you need to leave me alone."

We have had students get to this point. In fact, for my friend from the story earlier, that's where it ended. The bully put up some bluster, made some excuses, and walked away. But once they leave, everybody knows that they really didn't want to fight, they're not willing to back it up, and it becomes less fun, meaning the victim is no longer that weakest animal in the herd. It's time to find somebody easier.

What if the bully says "yes" and they do want to fight? And again, this is only really with the parents' permission; then it becomes time to use jujitsu. We only fight in the most nonviolent way possible. We only fight with the intention of subduing the other person and causing them to submit, to make them give up. So we teach our students to take the bully down very effectively. Hold them down, and if necessary, apply a submission technique to make them give up. We teach that we never injure the bully. We want to establish control and negotiate, which is part of Rule number 4.

Rule number four:

Never punch or kick the bully, include establish control and negotiate. Every time you punch or kick the bully, you will get in serious trouble. Guaranteed. Sometimes, in today's day and age, you may even get in trouble with law enforcement.

If you had a younger brother or sister, or if you had *any* brother or sister, you know that when they do something to you first and you hit them back, it seems like your parents always walk around the corner just in time to see the second person, and you end up getting in trouble. When you punch or kick the bully, even if they've been physically bullying you, you're likely to be the one who gets in trouble and falls prey to zero-tolerance.

Never punch or kick the bully. Only use your jujitsu techniques: establish control and negotiate. Now what does negotiate mean? We have a little running joke in our Bully Proof class that it does not mean, "Leave me alone or I will kill you." That's not negotiating. When we negotiate, we have to trade something, and what I'm going to trade is, "I will let you go if you promise to never touch me again."

Keep in mind that ideally this will be in range of other people seeing and hearing. If the bully wants to give up, to get up, or to be let out of this maybe somewhat painful submission technique, they need to submit, and they need to promise never to touch you again. Now, we always get the question from kids, "What if they get up and they attack you again?" You know what? That's a possibility, but once you proved that you can take them down and control them, it's unlikely they're going to want more of the same medicine.

Rule number five:

When applying submissions use minimal force and negotiate. So submissions are really only to be used as part of our psychological warfare against the bullies. They're there when the bully doesn't want to give up from being held down and they continue to resist giving in. Then we're allowed to use submissions.

We teach submissions like arm locks, shoulder locks, and basic techniques that can be painful and could be injurious. You could break somebody's arm with jujitsu, you could break somebody's shoulder, or you could choke somebody unconscious, but that's not what we teach the kids. We teach the kids to use them as a way to convince the bully that now is the time to give up.

The Rules: summarized

If you're reading this book, those five rules of engagement are absolutely critical to building up a kid's confidence, and it's twofold. We want the students obviously to have confidence to stand up for themselves. We want to give them the confidence that if they do, you'll be on their team. We teach the kids that if they run afoul of zero-tolerance, they should be very truthful and use the rules of engagement to explain what happened.

"Teacher, Derek has been bothering me and picking on me every day all year, and I've been asking for help and there's nobody that could help me. I need to speak to my mom or dad. I need to talk to my mom or dad." And then of course, we tell the kids that if they follow the rules of engagement, then you as the parents will be 100% in their court and go to bat for them.

We make no promises that they won't be suspended, but we do make the promise that they won't be in trouble at home for standing up for themselves. So we want them to have the confidence that if they needed to, they could stand up for themselves, and ultimately, as you saw in the other chapters, when the kids have that kind of confidence, then it rarely becomes necessary to use the actual self-defense techniques.

There's an old saying; "It's better to be a warrior in the garden than a gardener in a war," and that's so true. When you have the ability to actually defend yourself, then very often you don't need to. People can see, sense, and tell, that you're not somebody to be messed with and that you're not the weakest of the herd. That again is the best form of self-defense.

With that being said, I better take a step back for a moment and explain that with zero-tolerance, we understand kids who fight at school probably will get in trouble. The problem is that school is the place where the adults are the only people that can help you. Teachers and schools have a responsibility to take care of our kids. We give them our most precious possession for 6 or 8 hours a day. We trust them to take care of our kids.

As a side note: It's not a good idea for kids to schedule a fight after school. When you schedule a fight the bully inevitably brings friends, and that makes the process much more difficult and much more likely for the student to get hurt. And in school, if things go wrong, there is usually a grown up on the way to break up the fight. After school, there's no guarantee of help at all.

In fact, we have a parent whose child was in our Bully Proof class. He started getting picked on at school. The parent finally had enough after talking with the teachers and the other kid's parents. He tried everything that he could to get it to stop. And the parent said, "David, if that guy does that again, I want you to use jujitsu on him and take him down and make it stop, and I don't want you to wait till after school."

"It's better to do it now and get in trouble, than do it later and get hurt." And while we never encourage fighting, I agree with that sentiment 100%.

ZERO TOLERANCE

In this chapter, I want to talk about zero tolerance policies. I think the concept of zero tolerance is great. In fact, I have zero tolerance for bullying. But zero tolerance, like anything, can be taken to an extreme that makes it not effective for the purpose it was designed for. In reality, I think that's where many of our schools are at today.

I had a student not too long ago who came to our academy. He had been bullied in fourth grade, and this bullying consisted of psychological and some physical bullying in the form of poking, pinching, bothering, and things like that. He was getting lots of name calling and teasing. This student had been undergoing this bullying for an entire year in fourth grade. He was relieved to finally make it to summer and get away from the bully, only to have it renew again in fifth grade.

Halfway through the fifth-grade year, the bullying was still going on. A year and a half after being bullied incessantly, mom and dad talked to the school, the teacher, and even the other child's parents. But it was still going on. After a year and a half finally this student snapped, and he punched the other student in the face. Immediately both students were suspended for three days. Now, I don't know what kind of lesson that teaches kids when they're put in a situation where they have to go to school and they have to interact with these kids who are being mean. As far as the kid is concerned they are forced to be around a person who is bullying them day, after day, after day, after day, and nobody will help them. When they finally stand up for themselves, something that should be praised (although it would be better if they hadn't used physical force, or punching in particular), they get punished for it.

Compare that to the story of another student. He had been having trouble with a kid in 5th grade. They had conferences with the teachers and principal and things seemed to have been handled. Then in 6th grade, middle school, they ended up in the same gym class. About one month into the school year, the bully threw a volleyball at the student's head while he was playing with friends. It hit him, quite hard, in the back of the head. A few minutes later, the bully did it again, hitting the student in the head. The gym teacher was busy on his computer and didn't see what was happening. The THIRD time the bully threw the ball, my student was ready and caught the ball and threw it up on top of the bleachers where it would take few moments to get. The bully ran up to my student and shoved him to the ground. When the student got up, the bully shoved him down again.

As adults with the ability to stand up for ourselves, we would never allow someone to do that to us. We would stand up to them and either fight back or leave the situation. Many kids can't do that. They need the teachers to stand up for them. We depend on teachers to do that for our kids. That's why parents become so incensed when bullying continues to happen.

After being pushed down a second time, some of the student's friends came to his aid. One told the teacher, who intervened. The bully got taken to the principal's office and his parents were called. No further punishment that we are aware of. When the student's parents met with the teachers and principal, they were told that this was not a case of bullying and so there would be no suspension. There was not a pattern of behavior to make it bullying (never mind that the issues had been going on since the previous year!). Now, take a moment to consider that "zero-tolerance" punishment. He received a call to his parents and part of a day in the principal's office. If my student had gotten fed up with being hit in the head or shoved to the ground and punched the bully, they both would have been automatically suspended for 2 days in school suspension for fighting. It really seems like they had "zero-tolerance" for fighting back. They tolerate the bully until the victim can't tolerate it anymore. Then both the bully and the victim get in trouble. Who is hurt more by 2 days of suspension? The bully or the victim? Think of how many of these "victim fights back" incidents start. The victim may have been called names, teased, picked on, poked, touched, pushed, snickered at, gossiped about and more often for weeks, months, and even years. Many times a supervising adult was told, more than once of what was going on. All of that was tolerated. It was considered to be kids being kids. It happened to all of us when we were kids too, right? But finally, after such a long time of hating school and being afraid of the bully, the victim finally could not take it anymore and fought back. That CAN NOT be tolerated under the precepts of zero tolerance.

This might also explain another sad occurrence. We have a surprising number of kids that have been bullied so severely and for so long, that they end up transferring to a different school. Surely, if someone had to move, it should be the bully.

The concept of zero tolerance is absolutely right. There should be zero tolerance for bullying. However the reality is, and this is nothing against teachers, most people in general are very confrontation averse. People don't like confrontation. So when I see one kid poking another kid, I can totally understand how a teacher would be tempted to not call that bullying. Or when I hear a kid call another kid a name, I can totally understand how you would just tell them to knock it off and assume that it's regular kid stuff. I think a lot of the consistent nature of bullying can easily get swept under the rug as normal kid behavior, or one-off events, or a situation where both parties are at fault. The piece that's missing is the recognition of the continuing nature and the goal of the bullying.

I also believe, based on many years of experience teaching kids, that bullies are really, really smart about using zero tolerance in their benefit. The first way is very simple. Bullies know that the child being picked on is physically, emotionally, and mentally weaker than them. Or, at least they think this. They also know that the victim probably wants to follow the rules. They know the other child is not going to fight back because of zero tolerance. So, a good kid who desperately wants to follow the rules becomes aware of the consequences of zero tolerance and knows that if they stand up for themselves, they will get in trouble. Zero tolerance can cause kids (who maybe would have stood up for themselves) to just hunker down and endure the bullying longer, and longer, and longer. The bullies can use the zero-tolerance as a shield to protect themselves.

Often times zero tolerance is really not put into effect, at least by the upper administration, in order to help the kids, but more so because of a fear of lawsuits. If there's one thing that school administrators are afraid of, it's lawsuits. When students of ours are having trouble with bullying, we very much do not want them to fight; fighting is definitely only a last resort. But, what we do recommend is exactly what the school recommends. We recommend that they tell their parents, and we recommend that they tell the teacher. Usually after that's happened several times the parents will get in touch with the teacher as well and let them know. It's at this point where sometimes things go off the rails. Like I mentioned earlier, it's easy for some teachers to not recognize the regular nature or the continuing nature of the bullying,

They may also see it as the victim being too soft. Or, maybe they're over reacting to what's actually happening. They're being too sensitive. Maybe they just don't want to be confrontational. Maybe they know the bully's parents are going to throw a fit and have a big fight if they get called in. Don't get me wrong, many, many teachers are fantastic about dealing with bullies, and I highly recommend that you go directly to them. But, what we're talking about here is the cases where that didn't work. I recommend to our parents that if the teacher seems to not be solving the issue, then the parents should climb the ladder. If the teacher seems to not be taking it as seriously as you think they should, then you can talk to the principal. Generally in our experience, that's usually where it stops. The principals are more than a teacher, they're an administrator, and they're very aware and very afraid of lawsuits.

I'm not saying that we recommend that our parents threaten lawsuits, because we certainly don't. I don't think you have to. It's the nature of the world today that, when you explain that there's been bullying happening and it's not being solved, and you're tired of it, that often administrators are concerned with preventing lawsuits. If the principal isn't solving the issue, then go to the next level. Usually at some point you will find a level that is afraid of lawsuits, whether it's explicitly threatened or not. Which, again we don't recommend.

Ultimately, I think we've seen a lot of evidence that zero tolerance, while it can be helpful in stopping bullying, can also become a weapon for bullies to use against their victims, and they become very good at it. It can also be a shield. It's a shield for the school and the teachers that don't want to confront the bullying or the bully. It's a shield for them to hide behind and wait until the victim explodes and then use zero tolerance to justify how they're good at defending against bullying.

We are also hearing more and more about schools changing the name of their Zero Tolerance policy to something that sounds better. Or ultimately changing the rule to something else. However, the new names or new rules are often just a new coat of paint on the same problem. The policies still contain too much tolerance for the "kids being kids" and no tolerance for the victims standing up for themselves.

I think the vast majority of teachers have the best interest of all their students in mind, and they are heavily on the lookout for bullying. However, the ones that we're talking about today are the cases where the teachers can't or won't handle it.

Keep in mind that this chapter is about zero tolerance. A lot of bullying doesn't happen at school. It may happen before or after school. Often times it happens in places where it can't be proven or places where the teachers can't notice, such as in the bathroom, in a lunch line, or in the hallway. So, this is in no way condemning the vast majority of teachers, but as with every profession, there are always people who are less effective.

STATISTICS

I would be remiss if I didn't include a chapter on the statistics on bullying. As with most statistics, it's a bit of a mixed bag. There is some good news and some bad news. Some things are surprising and some are anticipated. More than anything, you should take away a deeper understanding of bullying and the issues surrounding it. Most of these statistics come directly from the United States Government website www.stopbullying.gov. There is a lot of great information there if you'd like to look into it more deeply.

I'll list some statistics with my thoughts sprinkled in. These are in no particular order.

- According to the National Center for Education Statistics, nearly **1 in 3** students (**27.8%**) report being bullied during the school year.
- If you were a victim of bullying, you may think that it's even higher than that. I mean, how many kids make

it to graduation without getting picked on for at least a short-term basis? On the other hand, you may think back to your childhood and think that it cannot really be that high. I don't know that's just what the studies say.

- The U.S. Department of Education and the U.S. Department of Justice Office of Justice Programs, reported that in 2015, about 5% of students ages 12–18 reported that they avoided at least one school activity or class or one or more places in school because they thought someone might attack or harm them.

Keep in mind that this fear is something that most of us as adults would never put up with. However, these kids feel that they can't get away from it. They feel that they can't get help. In their mind, the only escape is to pretend to be sick in order to stay home.

- Stopbullying.gov reported that over 70% of teenagers say they have witnessed bullying in their school.
- Wow. And this is with all of our bully prevention training at the schools and today's zero tolerance policies. There is some hope with this statistic though:
- When bystanders intervene, bullying stops within 10 seconds 57% of the time.
- First, it's pretty cool that they were able to get a statistic like that in the first place. And when you combine that with the previous number of 1 in 10, it kind of gives me hope. This book is about how to empower victims to stand up for themselves, but if we could get those witnesses to stand up too, we'd really be on to something big.

- According to the NEA, although the vast majority of school employees (**93%**) reported that their district had implemented a bullying prevention policy, just over half of all staff (**54%**) had received training related to the policy, and
- Over **80%** of school staff felt their district's policy was adequate.

This statistic from the NEA seems to be the weak link with our schools. Schools can do better. Teachers want to do better.

- The good news is, according to McCallion and Feder, school-based bullying prevention programs decrease bullying by up to **25%**.
- DoSomething.org stated that 1 out of every 10 kids who drop out of school does so because of repeated incidents of bullying.

That means it got so bad they couldn't take it any longer. It completely changes the entire trajectory of the rest of their life. AND that does not count the number of kids who transferred schools to get away from bullies. Especially in a larger city with multiple schools, this is amazingly common.

- 75% of shooting incidents at schools have been linked to bullying and harassment.

This is amazing. If none of the other statistics are doing it for you, this one should. If we could find a way to help these victims of bullying, we have the potential to influence 75% of school shooters.

- According to Zweig et al., the Urban Institute's study on bullying revealed that **17%** of bullying victims sought help after being victimized. Females were **twice** as likely to have sought help as males.

- The U.S. Department of Education and the U.S. Department of Justice Office of Justice Programs, reported that in 2011, students who reported being bullied notified an adult after being bullied only **40%** of the time and only **26%** of the time after being cyberbullied.

Kids often get the idea, rightly or wrongly, that no one can or will help them. Or that saying something about the bullying is being a snitch. This just drives home the importance of talking about it to your kids and making sure that they know you are in their corner.

Note: It is NEVER the victims fault that they are bullied. Everyone should be able to go to school and live their lives without fear of bullying. However, there are some common threads. Generally, children who are bullied have one or more of the following risk factors, according to StopBullying.gov:

- Are perceived as different from their peers, such as being overweight or underweight, wearing glasses or different clothing, being new to a school, or being unable to afford what kids consider "cool".
- Are perceived as weak or unable to defend themselves.
- Are depressed, anxious, or have low self-esteem.
- Are less popular than others and have few friends.
- Do not get along well with others, seen as annoying or provoking, or antagonize others for attention.

Signs and symptoms of bullying:

This is a list of things to be on the look out for. Any of these could certainly have other causes as well. But as parents, we owe it to our kids to be on the lookout.

Physical Symptoms:
- Unexplained bruises, scratches, and cuts
- Trouble sleeping or frequent nightmares
- Frequent headaches or stomach aches, feeling sick, or faking illness
- Changes in eating habits, like skipping meals or binge eating
- Lost or destroyed clothing, books, electronics, or jewelry

Behavioral and Psychological Symptoms:
- Loss of interest in school and extracurricular activities
- Feelings of helplessness, anxiety, or decreased self-esteem
- Seems sad, moody, or depressed
- Self-destructive behaviors (ex: cutting)
- Suicidal thoughts or ideas

Social Symptoms:
- Frequent complaints of illness to avoid attending school
- Sudden decrease in academic performance (declining grades or loss of interest)
- Fear of going to school, riding the bus, walking to school, or taking part in organized activities with other peers
- Sudden loss of friends or avoidance of social situations

When Bullying Occurs

Bully happens anywhere kids gather together in groups. The most common places to experience bullying are in school, outside on school grounds, and on the schools bus.

According to one large study, the following percentages of middle school students had experienced bullying in these various places at school: classroom (29.3%); hallway or lockers (29.0%); cafeteria (23.4%); gym or PE class (19.5%); bathroom (12.2%); playground or recess (6.2%).

While some of those numbers are surprising, and all of them are sad, there is a caveat. I will copy this directly from the United States Government website about bullying, as they put it succinctly:

Creating the impression that bullying is a bigger problem than it is spreads misinformation, which in media reports raises many ethical and professional concerns. Some experts contend that reports depicting bullying as widespread and rapidly grow-ing make youth and adults more likely to see it as common and less likely to try to stop it.

Adults accept it as part of growing up and think nothing can be done.

Youth think it is okay because "everyone does it."

Also, when people don't understand the actual dimension of a problem, they can make mistaken conclusions or even turn to the wrong solutions.

Finally, the idea that bullying is "everywhere" can contribute to irrational fears that can lead some to overprotective or anxious parenting. Some studies show that anxious parenting may harm children as they grow up.

We certainly don't want to overstate or sensationalize the problem. I think those last points are worth looking at again. Bullying affects up to 1 in 3 kids. But that means MOST kids don't get bullied. It would be wrong to assume that it's more than it really is. Everyone gets teased or name called now and then, and it's important to correctly identify bullying. This allows us to deal with it properly. Just like ignoring bullying is a problem, seeing bullying where there actually is none is also a serious issue.

CYBER BULLYING

We all remember what it was like to be picked on or teased when we were younger and now kids have to contend not only with that, but also the cyber bullying version. As technology becomes more present in our daily lives, it becomes more and more of a problem.

In a series of studies, 70-95% of kids in middle school said that they had been cyber bullied, so that means almost everybody is experiencing it to some degree. It seems like the anonymity of the internet, the ability to hide without people knowing your identity, allows people to say and do things that they would never normally say and do. It's even worse because we know that kids often are very mean to each other anyway, and then when you give them the ability to hide their identity and say anything they want without fear of repercussions, then cyber bullying can run rampant.

Now the flip side of that coin, another big part of the problem is that your kids won't tell you. Often, middle schoolers may be afraid to tell their parents if they are being cyber bullied, and this is a really important point for you to understand before it happens to your kid. They may fear that if they tell you about being cyber bullied you won't understand, that you will freak out, and that you will away their access to the technology or take away their access to the social media sites or apps that they were using.

Other times kids are too embarrassed by something that happened. Maybe they did or said something embarrassing or maybe there's pictures of them that are embarrassing or even pictures that they sent themselves that they don't want the parents to see. It's really, really important for you as a parent to understand that you have to let your kids know that you are not going to immediately freak out and take away their access to technology. They need to feel confident that they can talk to you without losing the access to all the things that they think are good about the technology.

They also need to understand that there are things that can be done about cyber bullying and it is part of the school's responsibility to help put an end to it, just as it is with physical forms of bullying. There are things that we can do to help our kids, but number one is we have to identify the problem, and if most kids are not going to tell their parents, then we need to act. Now I know that there's a lot of people out there who might disagree with this opinion, and maybe you're one of them, but I really truly believe that as a parent, we need to have the passwords to our kids' technology; we need to know where they're accessing the internet, and what apps and social media sites they're using, and we need to look at them.

We need to look for signs that they are being bullied. We need to look for signs that they're bullying, or participating, or that they're seeing it happening, and we even need to be a little bit of a sleuth and look for signs that they're deleting things, posts, and comments before you get a chance to see it. I really think that it would be a great idea once a week to sit down on the couch and go through your kid's phone and make sure there's nothing bad happening.

The importance of keeping up to date on what my kids are doing online became apparent to me when my daughter was 12. She is a very athletic, beautiful, and innocent child. She texted me and said, "Dad, do you think I could be a model?" Immediately, my red flags went up because why would somebody be talking to my daughter about being a model. I tried to stay level headed and I asked her what she was talking about. She said, "Well, I'm on this app and this guy saw some of my pictures and said that I could be a model."

Immediately, I became very leery, as we know online there's a lot of people trolling for kids, pretending to be agents or pretending to be other kids. In reality, they're 40-year-old men who are planning who knows what. I told her, "Hey, don't respond and let me come home and look at it." By then he had followed up again with, "You know, you could really make some money," and he made an implication that maybe they could work something out and the next step was an offer to meet. He was fairly aggressive about it, even after she had stopped replying.

I'm very thankful that she asked me not realizing what was happening and afterwards I became very afraid. A 12 year old is too innocent and inexperienced with the harsh realities of the real world to have to suspect that anyone online could be out to get them. But that is the way it is. And even if they suspect something isn't right, they are too young to know the best ways of dealing with these situations. We had a long discussion about how people online will use the fact that you can't see them to claim to be something they are not. Like a 40-year-old man claiming to be a 12-year-old boy or some basement dweller claiming to be from a modeling agency. I trust my daughter very much, but I still worry that she does not have the experience and maturity to handle every possible situation. I think the same thing with bullying, so now I make it a point once a week to take a look at my kid's phone. Sometimes I do it with them sitting next to me and other times I do it with them not. I tell them it's important that I know their passwords and because of that they should simply live their lives in a way where they don't say things online that they would not say to another person's face.

Now what do we do when we find out that our child is being cyber bullied? A little bit of it depends on whether it's anonymous or whether you're able to identify the bullies. If you're able to identify them, then taking the route of the school and the police really is the way to go. It's best not to engage on social media. It's very hard to defeat a keyboard ninja in his home domain, but when you can identify the perpetrator, then you have avenues to make it stop.

When it becomes a real challenge is when you can't identify the bully when it's anonymous. It's really important if you are having trouble like that to make sure that you screenshot it and record everything that you possibly can, and then if you deem it necessary, contact the police.

Unlike when we were kids and we could get away from people or bullies at school, our kids go home from school and they can continue to be bullied online. The weekend comes along and instead of getting away from it for the weekend, it accelerates and gets worse and worse through online conversations and communication.

Kids can find that there is no escape, and tragically, we've even seen a rise in cyber bullying related suicides. It really is a critical form of bullying to understand and the number one most important thing is for parents to be aware and to find out when it's happening so that they can help their kids because the kids, especially in this case, won't always ask for our help.

ACTION STEPS

Throughout the book, we've detailed some information to help deal with bullying and how to help your kids, but I want to take the chapter and really just boil it down step by step. Number one is to identify the problem. Pay attention to your kid's behavior, grades, actions, and attitudes, and make sure you can identify if something's going on. Make sure to have open lines of communication with them and talk to them so that when or if something does happen, you'll be aware.

But once you've identified that bullying is going on, you can always contact the other kid's parents. Now, some people have success with that and some people don't. Maybe in the old days, it was better. I think the danger nowadays of contacting the other parents directly is that there are many parents that see their kid as the perfect little angel who can't do any wrong and needs to be defended at all costs against any slanders. Unless you know the other parents, we don't really recommend that you go direct to them.

The first stop would be the school, your kid's teacher at school first. Then, the principal likely would need to be involved. Of course, if this is not happening at school, maybe the teacher or supervisor, whoever's in charge of your child. In today's day and age, they should be trained how to deal with bullying. This is also the time to look for a good martial arts academy. Developing the confidence and skills to stand up for themselves does not happen over night. Do not wait until the bullying has been going on so long that your child can not take it any longer. Be proactive. Do your homework and exhaust every avenue you can to help them take control of the situation.

One of my kids had an incident at school where another kid smacked him upside the head. We talked to the principal and we felt that the principal handled it very, very well, and they came to what we felt was a good resolution as the school administration. Now oftentimes, that's all it will take. I don't want to make it sound like the schools are not doing a good job because most teachers and most administrators really do care about their kids and they really do take bullying seriously.

However, sometimes that doesn't work. It may be a case where you need to go to the police and to see if they can help. In my experience very often with kids bullying each other, the police hands are kind of tied and they're not able to help as much as you would wish. If you feel like your school is not solving the problem appropriately, then seek the next level, a superintendent perhaps or the school board. Oftentimes, if you get an attorney involved and, of course, this is like worst case scenario, schools become very fearful of lawsuits and can absolutely be spurred into action if they hadn't been taking action before.

I would say number one, go to the teacher. Number two,

talk to the principal. Then number three would be to involve the police or maybe the school liaison officer. After exhausting all of those avenues, then perhaps getting an attorney. Now as we talked about in previous chapters, in real life, sometimes there is nobody else to help you and you'll need to coach your child to stand up for themselves. If you have an opportunity to train in martial arts, it'll be a tremendous benefit, but sometimes even just standing up for yourself no matter the outcome can be enough to change the situation. Of course, your advice to your children to stand up for themselves is very dependent on your kid, their personality, what the bullies are doing, and how many bullies there are. So that's not really a blanket answer for everyone, but if the situation warrants it, that would really be the worst case or the last resort.

CONCLUSION

B y way of conclusion, I have helped probably hundreds of kids that started martial arts because they were having problems with bullies. Many of them were helped simply by learning to be good at a skill and developing confidence and self esteem in themselves to maybe just not care so much when other people say something. Other kids trained in martial arts until they developed the confidence to actually stand up to the bully, look them in the eye, and say, "You need to stop." It's only been a very, very small number of people who needed to stand up and physically fight the bully. In fact, it is very, very rare.

In the past 15 years of teaching, I've taught thousands and thousands of kids and I would guess that only a small handful have ever physically had to fight a bully. I'm sure it does happen and it's probably happened after kids left our academy or that I didn't hear about but it's very uncommon. By far, the biggest form of self defense is having confidence in yourself. There is no better activity for developing and training a person's confidence than a quality martial arts academy. For parents, I suggest visiting a quality martial arts academy that's going to help you develop that confidence that's necessary in today's world for not only standing up to bullies but also having the ability to stand out and to show the world what you're made of.

Thank you for taking the time to read my book. I encourage you to reach out to me anytime for advice on bullying or how our martial arts classes can help with your specific situation.

EXCELLENCE

onus chapter, excellence. So this book has been totally about bullying, and partly about how martial arts can help your child defeat bullies by having the confidence to stand up for themselves, physically if necessary. But I wanted to make this bonus chapter to give you just one of the other tremendous benefits that I see from martial arts training.

One of them goes back to an old saying, and I'm not sure where it came from to give credit where credit is due, but the saying is, "You are the average of the five people that you spend the most time with." And what that means is if you spend time hanging out with pessimistic people, or low achievers, or people who set their goals low, and don't have ambition, then they tend to drag you down in that direction. But if you surround yourself with high achievers, and people who are ambitious, work hard, and set their goals high, and strive for excellence in everything they do, then they will pull you and rise you up so that you have many of the same attributes.

I just want to point out how in many cases, the public schools and even the private schools, the schools in general, are not always providing your kids with the five best people for them to be surrounded with. We all want our kids to be happy and successful, to have integrity, and to be good people when they grow up. By joining martial arts, a quality martial arts academy, your child is immediately surrounded by people who are striving for those same things. People who train in martial arts, or have their kids train, are ambitious. They want success and they want their kids to be happy. These people want to have integrity, discipline, and respect. By simply being surrounded by those people, it makes your child strive for greater levels of excellence.

In addition to that, when you've been at a martial arts academy for any length of time, your child will start to make friends with the students in class. At our academy we have students who are trained two, three, four, five, even seven, 10 years, and they develop close relationships with other kids that they've been in class with, many times for years.

Often times they get to know the kids from their martial arts academy better than most of the kids they know at school. And any child who has been in martial arts three or four years, obviously has discipline and respect and integrity, and is, at least, working hard to accomplish some really big goals. That's all we want for our kids, right? We want our kids to be the best that they can be. We want them to be the happiest that they can be and doing what they want in life. We don't want our kids to be stuck going to work at a low-end job, working 40, 50, 60 hours, going home, watch an hour of TV, go to bed, and get up and do it again.

Success coach Jim Rohn says, "You are the average of the five people you spend the most time with." You have little to no control over who your child hangs out with at school. Some are probably good kids, but others…not so much. By being involved in a great martial arts academy, you can ensure that your child is spending time around, being influence by, and becoming friends with other high achievers. Your child will spend a lot of time training with other kids that expect to get good grades, expect to go to a great college or start a business, and expect to work hard and be disciplined even when the teacher isn't watching.

Then in addition, you give them the role models of the instructors. Instructors, of course, are normal human beings with flaws like anybody else, but they're always striving to be better. They're striving to be an example of discipline and respect. Unlike other sports athletes, your martial arts instructors understand that they are on a pedestal. They understand that they are role models. The kids do look up to them, and they need to do their best to live up to those standards. Excellence is another tremendous side effect of choosing the right martial arts academy, and hopefully you'll be able to find one that will fit you and help you accomplish greatness for your child. I tell our students: "I am only truly fulfilled when I am using my talents and skills to their fullest extent."

ABOUT THE AUTHOR

Ryan has always loved martial arts. Inspired by the Ninja Turtles, He-man and GI Joe he started his martial arts journey when he was 8 years old. In his teens he realized his desire to teach others the same lessons he had learned in training. Ryan went to Iowa State University for Mechanical Engineering, but after 3 years, realized his true calling. He graduated with a degree in business and went on to open his own martial arts academy. Since then he has trained thousands of students in martial arts. He also enjoys training others in Leadership skills and especially helping kids develop the confidence to stand up to bullies.

Ryan lives in Sioux City, IA. He has four kids that keep him busy. He enjoys teaching, reading and training. Feel free to look him up on facebook or other social media to see what he's up to currently.

Made in the USA
Columbia, SC
31 January 2018